40 Days of Prayer

For Grieving Parents

Cindy Shufflebarger

ISBN 978-0-9850049-4-1

Dear Friend, I am so sorry for your loss and my heart hurts for you. I, too, have lived through the grief ushered in by the death of a child. We meet here where no one wants to meet. Yet, my prayer is that you encounter God in a new way over the next forty days as you pray your way through these pages. May your hope be renewed. May you feel the love of our heavenly Father. May you find rest for your weary soul.

You are brave to be here in this space. Maybe you feel lost or alone or simply desperate. Whatever brought you here, may you find God who loves you with an unending, perfect love. Dare to explore who he is. Dare to invite him into the wounds and grief. Dare to expose your broken heart. He will show up with healing salve for your heart, your mind, and your soul. The journey is not easy, but walking with him will provide you the strength and power to move forward and to find joy again.

As Brother Lawrence reminds us, "Let us occupy ourselves entirely in knowing God. The more we know Him, the more we will desire to know Him. As love increases with knowledge, the more we know God, the more we will truly love Him. We will learn to love Him equally in times of distress or in times of great joy." Healing begins in his presence. Join him and invite him to show you the way.

Prayers and blessings,

Cindy

HOW TO MAKE THE MOST OF THIS JOURNAL

Find a quiet place and begin with a simple prayer asking God to give you insight, wisdom, and direction about the passage and prompts.

VERSE:
Read the verse and consider the characteristics of God it reveals.

PRAYER:
Read the prayer and let it be a springboard for your thoughts and conversation with God. Personalize it beyond the written words.

GOD IS:
Look for words in the verse that describe God or point to one of his characteristics. Use this section to consider his myriad attributes and how different aspects of his character may be especially helpful to you right now.

SOMETHING I'M THANKFUL FOR:
Use this space for praise and thanksgiving. List attributes of God that you recognize and appreciate. Or, give thanks for people, provisions, situations, opportunities, solutions, and answers to prayer.

TRUTH TO PONDER:
Use this as a focal point for your day. Consider how it applies to you currently and how you can view your grief in context of God's truth.

PRAYERS AND REFLECTIONS:
Use the prompts to write a prayer and/or thoughts about the verse or your feelings for the day. You can use bullet points, full sentences, or simply make notes. Always feel free to go back and add thoughts to a particular day. Consider looking back through previous pages periodically to read responses and see how God is working in this season of prayer and grief. Add a date somewhere on the page if that's helpful to you.

MORE VERSES:
The verses listed in this section offer additional examples and context for the daily focus. They are not an exhaustive list, so feel free to look for others that apply. Taking time to look them up, either on a Bible app or a hard copy of the Bible, will enrich your quiet time. Make notes about what they mean and specific words or phrases that speak to you. Consider how God is revealing different aspects of himself through various verses.

SAMPLE:
The following two pages show a sample of how to complete the sections.

Since, then, you have been raised with Christ, set your hearts on things above... Set your minds on things above, not on earthly things. Colossians 3:1-2

Prayer

Lord, Direct my thoughts. Help me stay focused on you - your truth, your promises, your goodness. Shift my thoughts when they wander. Lord, I love you and want to praise you. Remind me of all the ways you're good. Show me your goodness today. In Jesus' name I ask. Amen.

According to this verse, God is...

powerful (raised Jesus, and saved me)

greater than earthly things

Something I'm thankful for today:

beautiful fall weather

a phone call from a friend

Truth to Ponder

When I'm focused on God's goodness, my heart and mind experience relief from my pain.

Prayers & Reflections

Lord, I feel...

overwehelmed and confused, I can't quite figure out what to do nept. I dont want to get stuck here, but I can't see the nept step.

Lord, I choose to think about...

you loved me enough to send Jesus. you promise to be faithful, true, unchanging. your word says you're good - a good father, a good shepherd.

More Verses: Philippians 4:8, 2 Corinthians 4:18

The Lord is close to the brokenhearted and saves those who are crushed in spirit. Psalm 34:18

Prayer

Lord, Be near and bring healing to my broken heart. I struggle to imagine my life moving forward. Comfort me. Give me peace. Help me to see you and feel your presence. Give me a desire to want to get up in the morning and give me strength to put one foot in front of the other as I walk the path before me. Help me, Lord. Amen

According to this verse, God is...

Something I'm thankful for today:

Truth to Ponder

God loves me. Always. My circumstances and feelings are not an indicator of his love for me.

Prayers & Reflections

Lord, I feel...

Lord, Help me...

More Verses: Psalm 147:3, Isaiah 61:1

Come to me, all who labor and are heavy laden, and I will give you rest. Take my yoke upon you, and learn from me, for I am gentle and lowly in heart, and you will find rest for your souls.
Matthew 11:28-29

Prayer

Lord, I need your rest. My grief feels heavy and suffocating. I need you to lift my burdens and carry the weight. Please show me your goodness and grace. Give me hope and grant me peace. In Jesus' name I ask. Amen.

According to this verse, God is...

Something I'm thankful for today:

Truth to Ponder

God understands my grief and offers rest. He can carry the load of my overwhelming emotions.

Prayers & Reflections

Lord, I feel...

Lord, Show me your truth about...

More Verses: Exodus 33:14, Psalm 62:1-2 (NIV)

My flesh and my heart may fail, but God is the strength of my heart and my portion forever.
Psalm 73:26

Prayer

Dear Father, Help me to see the depths of your love for me and to understand the power of your strength. I want to trust you, but my heart is hurting. Equip me. Encourage me. Give me eyes to see all the ways you provide and are present with me. Strengthen my heart, my mind, and my body as I experience the effects of grief and loss. Amen.

According to this verse, God is...

Something I'm thankful for today:

Truth to Ponder

God's strength will sustain me.

Prayers & Reflections

Lord, I feel...

Lord, I praise you because...

More Verses: Psalm 61:2, Psalm 63:1-8

My soul is weary with sorrow; strengthen me according to your word.
Psalm 119:28

Prayer

Lord, Your word says you love me. Your word says you're all-powerful and good. Your word says you can do all things. Nothing is too hard for you. Help me to believe these truths. Help me to trust you with my emotions and circumstances. Lord, strengthen me physically, emotionally and spiritually. I need you desperately.
In Jesus' name I pray. Amen.

According to this verse, God is...

Something I'm thankful for today:

Truth to Ponder

God's word is powerful truth.

Prayers & Reflections

Lord, I feel...

Lord, I'm wrestling with these thoughts...

More Verses: Isaiah 41:10, Psalm 23:4, Zephaniah 3:17

Be merciful to me, Lord, for I am in distress; my eyes grow weak with sorrow, my soul and body with grief. Psalm 31:9

Prayer

I ache with longing. Fill the empty spaces within me. I need your love, your grace, your comfort, your strength. Show me the way toward rest and healing. Settle me with your peace and presence. Comfort me with your love and surround me with your compassion. Amen.

According to this verse, God is...

Something I'm thankful for today:

Truth to Ponder

Grief impacts the body physically and emotionally. Allow yourself the space to grieve and lean into God's grace.

Prayers & Reflections

Lord, I feel...

Lord, Help me...

More Verses: Psalm 57:1, Hebrews 4:16

This is my comfort in my affliction, that your promise gives me life.
Psalm 119:50

Prayer

Lord, I need you. I can't do this alone. Remind me of your promises. Remind me of your love and goodness. Let me hear your truth today and fill my aching spirit with hope. Provide exactly what I need today and remind me that you are near. Amen.

According to this verse, God is...

Something I'm thankful for today:

Truth to Ponder

God is trustworthy. He keeps his promises. His word (the Bible) is truth.

Prayers & Reflections

Lord, I feel...

Lord, Help me focus on the following promises:

More Verses: Psalm 19:7, Isaiah 43:2, Proverbs 3:5-6

May the God of hope fill you with all joy and peace in believing, so that by the power of the Holy Spirit you may abound in hope. Romans 15:13

Prayer

Lord, Fear overtakes me at times. Fear that I won't know joy again. Fear that I can't live life without my child. Fear that I will be stuck here forever, yet fear of moving ahead. Lord, I need your hope. I can't imagine what that even looks like some days, but you know exactly what I need. Please show me. In Jesus' name I ask. Amen.

According to this verse, God is...

Something I'm thankful for today:

Truth to Ponder

Hope is not found in things of this world, but in God's power and the promise of his presence.

Prayers & Reflections

Lord, I feel...

I have hope because...

More Verses: 1 Peter 5:10, Hebrews 10:23, Isaiah 40:31

The Lord is my strength and my song, and he has become my salvation; this is my God, and I will praise him, my father's God, and I will exalt him. Exodus 15:2

Prayer

Lord, I praise you as my loving Father. I struggle to understand your ways, but I trust that you see the bigger picture and will redeem my pain. Comfort me. Show me your grace. Make me aware of your presence and love. Calm my fears and restore my joy. May I remember your goodness and praise you for who you are. I love you. Amen.

According to this verse, God is...

Something I'm thankful for today:

Truth to Ponder

When I feel stuck in my grief, praise and worship will shift my attention to God, giving me moments of relief.

Prayers & Reflections

Lord, I feel...

How I saw evidence of God this week:

More Verses: Psalm 145: 3, Revelation 4:11, Psalm 63:3-4

Casting all your anxieties on him, Because he cares for you. 1 Peter 5:7

Prayer

Lord, Show me how to cast my pain and fear on you. I want you to carry the burden so I can feel a little lighter. Help me to see that you care. I want your healing and truth to permeate my life. I am weary and need your strength, comfort, and understanding. Help me to see beauty in this day and trust that you are with me in this journey of grief. Amen.

According to this verse, God is...

Something I'm thankful for today:

Truth to Ponder

God offers peace and comfort in exchange for our pain when we freely release it to him.

Prayers & Reflections

Lord, I feel...

Lord, I am anxious about...

More Verses: Psalm 119:76, Proverbs 3:24, Matthew 5:4

Because of the Lord's great love we are not consumed, for his compassions never fail. They are new every morning; great is your faithfulness.
Lamentations 3:22-23

Prayer

Lord, Thank you for a new day. I invite your grace and mercy for all that is ahead of me. My reality of sorrow and pain still envelopes me. Sustain me in this day as I move ahead. Lead me. Encourage me. Fill me with hope when I cannot see a clear path to healing. Show me your compassion and let me experience your faithfulness in this day. Amen.

According to this verse, God is...

Something I'm thankful for today:

Truth to Ponder

God is compassionate and loves us more than we can imagine. He demonstrated the depths of his love for us on the cross.

Prayers & Reflections

Lord, I feel...

How I've seen evidence of God's love for me in the past week:

More Verses: Psalm 147:3, John 3:16, 2 Corinthians 1:3-4

Through him then let us continually offer up a sacrifice of praise to God, that is, the fruit of lips that acknowledge his name. Hebrews 13:15

Prayer

Lord, Today my praise is an intentional act of worship. It is a step of faith. I praise you because you are worthy of praise, not because I feel like it. Please accept my offering of praise, my expression of love for you and help my feelings to follow. You are sovereign, mighty, gracious, loving and good. You are the Good Shepherd, the Bread of Life and Living Water. Nourish my soul today as I praise you. Amen.

According to this verse, God is...

Something I'm thankful for today:

Truth to Ponder

Praising God for who he is, despite our pain, paves a path to healing.

Prayers & Reflections

Lord, I feel...

Lord, I need ...

More Verses: Psalm 145:1, Revelation 4:11, Psalm 150:6

The Lord is gracious and righteous;
our God is full of compassion.
Psalm 116:5

Prayer

Loving Father, I need to feel your compassion today. Please show me evidence that you see me and care about my grief and heartache. Whether it's through a person, scripture, something beautiful you created, or words of encouragement from someone I encounter today, please make it abundantly clear that you love me and are near.
In Jesus' name I pray. Amen.

According to this verse, God is...

Something I'm thankful for today:

Truth to Ponder

When we invite God to draw near, he responds with compassion.

Prayers & Reflections

Lord, I feel...

I felt encouraged this week when...

More Verses: Psalm 145:18, Isaiah 41:10

Restore our fortunes, Lord, like streams in the Negev. Those who sow with tears will reap with songs of joy. Those who go out weeping, carrying seed to sow, will return with songs of joy, carrying sheaves with them. Psalm 126:4-6

Prayer

Lord, I struggle to comprehend returning from this season of grief with a song of joy. But Lord, I ask you to give me the courage to trust you and sing your praises as I endure this heartache. Show me that you are greater than my sorrow. Show me that you redeem and restore. Show me that you will bring something beautiful out of my devastation. Lord, only you are capable of such transformation. Give me eyes to see and a heart to believe. Amen.

According to this verse, God is...

Something I'm thankful for today:

Truth to Ponder

God can turn ashes into beauty, pain into hope, and tears into joy. Nothing is too hard for him.

Prayers & Reflections

Lord, I feel...

Lord, Help me ...

More Verses: Isaiah 61:3, Romans 8:28, Psalm 23:5

Jesus wept.
John 11:35

Prayer

Lord, Thank you for the reminder that you understand my sorrow and pain. You were fully human and experienced grief in many ways - grief from the loss of a loved one, grief from insults, grief from rejection and from persecution. I know you understand and I thank you for your willingness to sit with me in my sadness. Please comfort me and remind me of your love. Amen.

According to this verse, God is...

Something I'm thankful for today:

Truth to Ponder

Jesus understands our grief.

Prayers & Reflections

Lord, I feel...

It comforts me when...

More Verses: Matthew 26:38, Matthew 27:46, Hebrews 4:15

Answer me, O Lord, for your steadfast love is good; according to you abundant mercy, turn to me, Hide not your face from your servant, for I am in distress; make haste answer me. Psalm 69:16-17

Prayer

Lord, I feel alone as I sit in my grief. No one can do the work for me and at times I am overwhelmed with emotion. Please remind me of your goodness. Fill my thoughts with your loving promises. Reveal yourself to me in a way that brings comfort and hope. I need you. Amen.

According to this verse, God is...

Something I'm thankful for today:

Truth to Ponder

God responds when we invite him into our grief.

Prayers & Reflections

Lord, I feel...

How I've experienced God's presence this week:

More Verses: Psalm 50:15, Jeremiah 33:3, Psalm 91:15

Be still and know that I am God.

Psalm 46:10

Prayer

Loving Father, I am unsettled about so many things. My feelings swing, my thoughts are scattered. Please calm me. Help me to be still and rest in you. Remind me of all the reasons I can trust you with my circumstances and my pain. Remind me of your power and sovereignty over all. Overwhelm me with your love and gentleness. May I exhale and rest in you right now. Amen.

According to this verse, God is...

Something I'm thankful for today:

Truth to Ponder

God sees me, knows me, and loves me.

Prayers & Reflections

Lord, I feel...

Lord, Help me to be still and fully trust you with the following:

More Verses: Ephesians 3:20, Hebrews 7:25, Jeremiah 32:27

He will wipe away every tear from their eyes, and death shall be no more, neither shall there be mourning, nor crying, nor pain anymore, for the former things have passed away. Revelation 21:4

Prayer

Dear Gracious Father, Thank you for the promise of eternity with you in heaven. Help me to embrace the truth of this verse. Oh, how I miss my child and struggle to imagine an end to my mourning. Bring peace and comfort. Show me that you are bigger than all my pain and sadness. Turn my ashes into beauty even though I can't comprehend what that might look like. Give me hope and a vision of your glory. Amen.

According to this verse, God is...

Something I'm thankful for today:

Truth to Ponder

Focusing on God's promises for the future shifts our perspective.

Prayers & Reflections

Lord, I feel...

Lord, Help me understand...

More Verses: Isaiah 25:8-9, Revelation 7:16-17

Give thanks to the Lord, for he is good, for his steadfast love endures forever.
Psalm 136:1

Prayer

Lord, I struggle to see your goodness in my grief. Open my eyes to your truth. Give me the courage to trust you. Reveal your love for me and reassure me when I doubt. Nothing is too hard for you and I invite you to work in my thought life and guide my emotions. In Jesus' name I ask. Amen.

According to this verse, God is...

Something I'm thankful for today:

Truth to Ponder

God loves me even when I don't feel it. He has a good plan for me even when I don't see it.

Prayers & Reflections

Lord, I feel...

Lord, I know you love me because...

More Verses: 1 John 3:1, John 10:10

Do not let your hearts be troubled. You believe in God; believe also in me. My Father's house has many rooms; if that were not so, would I have told you that I am going there to prepare a place for you? John 14:1-2

Prayer

Father, Thank you that you are preparing an eternal place for me. Thank you for inviting me into your family. Thank you that I'll experience your joy and presence forever. Remind me when I lose sight of the hope I have. Settle my heart and mind. Make your presence known to me today and remind me of all the blessings I have as your child. May I not forget your goodness and love. Amen.

According to this verse, God is...

Something I'm thankful for today:

Truth to Ponder

We have eternity in heaven to anticipate. We will experience complete perfection and unending joy one day.

Prayers & Reflections

Lord, I feel...

Lord, I praise you because...

More Verses: Psalm 16:11, Philippians 4:4, Psalm 30:5

Evening and morning and noon I utter my complaint and moan, and he hears my voice.
Psalm 55:17

Prayer

Lord, You know my heart and my thoughts before I utter a word to you. When I don't know what to ask, intervene on my behalf. I need you. Please show me that you see and hear me. Encourage me in a tangible way. Remind me of your faithfulness. I ask in Jesus' name. Amen.

According to this verse, God is...

Something I'm thankful for today:

Truth to Ponder

God hears my cries. Even though I may not see it, he is working on my behalf.

Prayers & Reflections

Lord, I feel...

Lord, Help me...

More Verses: Psalm 145:18, Psalm 34:17, 1 John 5:14-15

The one who offers thanksgiving as his sacrifice glorifies me; to one who orders his way rightly I will show the salvation of God! Psalm 50:23

Prayer

Loving Father, I thank you for all the ways you demonstrate your love for me. Thank you for the gift of salvation. Thank you for your grace, mercy, and forgiveness. Thank you for the time I got to spend with my child. Thank you that you use the hard things to shape me and draw me to you. I don't understand your ways, but I thank that you love me and that you will redeem and restore even the most bitter things in my life when I allow you to do your work. Amen.

According to this verse, God is...

Something I'm thankful for today:

Truth to Ponder

Gratitude opens a door to focus on God instead of our pain. It is a powerful tool in healing.

Prayers & Reflections

Lord, I feel...

Ways I can practice gratitude in spite of my grief:

More Verses: 1 Thess 5:16-18, Psalm 9:1, 1 Chronicles 16:8

And we know that in all things God works for the good of those who love him, who have been called according to his purpose. Romans 8:28

Prayer

Lord, I struggle to see the good in my situation right now. Give me the courage and willingness to consider that something good might emerge from the pain of my loss. Be patient with me. Be gentle with me. But fill me with hope and purpose. I desire your best, and I ask for your grace to see and receive it. In Jesus' name I ask it. Amen.

According to this verse, God is...

Something I'm thankful for today:

Truth to Ponder

God has a good plan and purpose even for the most painful pieces of my life.

Prayers & Reflections

Lord, I feel...

How I've felt encouraged this week:

More Verses: Job 42:2, Psalm 138:8, Isaiah 14:24

For our light and momentary troubles are achieving for us an eternal glory that far outweighs them all. So we fix our eyes not on what is seen, but on what is unseen, since what is seen is temporary, but what is unseen is eternal. 2 Corinthians 4:17-18

Prayer

Lord, My troubles seem very heavy and overwhelming. Help me to see how your glory and goodness can make my afflictions seem temporary. While this may be truth, I struggle to feel it. Show me how to fix my gaze on you. Show me how to praise you despite my pain. Show me how to have faith and hope in light of my devastating loss. I need you, Lord. Be near. In Jesus' I pray. Amen.

According to this verse, God is...

Something I'm thankful for today:

Truth to Ponder

When we fix our eyes on Jesus, our perspective changes.

Prayers & Reflections

Lord, I feel...

Lord, Help me shift my thoughts related to:

More Verses: Romans 8:35-39, 1 Peter 4:13, Philippians 4:13

Peace I leave with you; my peace I give you. I do not give as the world gives. Do not let your hearts be troubled and do not be afraid. John 14:27

Prayer

Lord, Thank you for offering your peace to me. I need it as I am overcome with worry and uncertainty. My emotions rage and my security seems rocked by the loss of my child. Calm my fears. Settle my anxious heart. Daily remind me of the promise of your peace in the midst of my chaos. Thank you for loving me and for guiding me as I try to make sense of my grief. Be my anchor and reorient me to your truth as I sift and sort my feelings. Amen.

According to this verse, God is...

Something I'm thankful for today:

Truth to Ponder

I can choose to accept Jesus' offer of peace.

Prayers & Reflections

Lord, I feel...

Lord, I need your peace about...

More Verses: Philippians 4:6-7, Psalm 4:8, Romans 8:6

Have I not commanded you? Be strong and courageous. Do not be afraid; do not be discouraged, for the Lord your God will be with you wherever you go. Joshua 1:9

Prayer

Lord, Make me aware of your presence. I know that you're everywhere, but it doesn't feel like it right now. Show me evidence of your presence. Make it clear to me that you love me and see me. I need your reassurance right now. Please be real to me today and do what it takes to get my attention. In Jesus' name I ask. Amen.

According to this verse, God is...

Something I'm thankful for today:

Truth to Ponder

God is with me. Right now. Always.

Prayers & Reflections

Lord, I feel...

Lord, I feel your presence when...

More Verses: Exodus 33:14, Jeremiah 29:13, Psalm 139:7

Bless the Lord, O my soul and all that is within me, bless his holy name! Bless the Lord, O my soul, and forget not all his benefits. Psalm 103:1-2

Prayer

Lord, You are worthy of praise even when I'm feeling sad and down. You have blessed me in so many ways, may I not forget. You have created me, loved me, saved me. You are my salvation and my hope. You invite me into your presence and offer your peace, comfort and rest. May I accept your mercy and grace and hold confidently to the promises of your goodness and love. Amen.

According to this verse, God is...

Something I'm thankful for today:

Truth to Ponder

God loves me, chose me, and calls me his child. I will spend eternity with him.

Prayers & Reflections

Lord, I feel...

Lord, I praise you because...

More Verses: Ephesians 1:3-5, Psalm 5:11-12, Galatians 3:29

O Lord, be gracious to us; we wait for you. Be our arm every morning, our salvation in the time of trouble. Isaiah 33:2

Prayer

Lord, Encourage me as I wait. Point my eyes toward you. Strengthen me for I am weary. Comfort my hurting heart. Fill my thoughts with your hope and truth. Father, I need to be reminded of your power and your ability to redeem all things. Show me the depths of your love.
In Jesus' name I ask. Amen.

According to this verse, God is...

Something I'm thankful for today:

Truth to Ponder

God is working while I'm waiting.

Prayers & Reflections

Lord, I feel...

Lord, I believe you are good because...

More Verses: Jeremiah 32:17, Hebrews 4:16, Luke 1:45

Continue steadfastly in prayer, being watchful in it with thanksgiving. Colossians 4:2

Prayer

Lord, Thank you for the work you're doing in my life right now. Bring healing and restoration. Show me your ways. Open my eyes to your presence. Grace me with perspective to see beyond my circumstances. I praise you for who you are and I trust that your ways are better than mine. Remind me that you're in control and that you work all things together for good for those who love you. In Jesus's name I ask. Amen

According to this verse, God is...

Something I'm thankful for today:

Truth to Ponder

Daily gratitude paves a path to healing.

Prayers & Reflections

Lord, I feel...

Lord, I am patiently waiting for...

More Verses: 1 Thessalonians 5:16-18, Romans 12:12

From the end of the earth I call to you when my heart is faint. Lead me to the rock that is higher than I. Psalm 61:2

Prayer

Lord, My heart is faint and I'm calling to you. Lift me. Give me strength to do the things before me today. Give me courage to step toward the future. Lift my eyes toward you and secure me with your strong arms of protection. Thank you for your love and comfort. Amen.

According to this verse, God is...

Something I'm thankful for today:

Truth to Ponder

God will supply me with the strength I need for today.

Prayers & Reflections

Lord, I feel...

Lord, Hear my cry for:

More Verses: John 16:33, Psalm 121:1-2, Isaiah 41:10

And after you have suffered a little while, the God of all grace, who has called you to his eternal glory in Christ, will himself restore, confirm, strengthen, and establish you. 1 Peter 5:10

Prayer

Lord, Relieve my pain and suffering. It wasn't supposed to be this way and I will always miss my child. I don't even want to move on in this life without them. But I also don't want to stay in this place of agony. So, in your way and in your time, I ask you to restore and heal my broken heart. Amen.

According to this verse, God is...

Something I'm thankful for today:

Truth to Ponder

Restoration and healing are possible.

Prayers & Reflections

Lord, I feel...

Lord, I need...

More Verses: Isaiah 43:2, James 1:12, Romans 8:26

And I am sure of this, that he who began a good work in you will bring it to completion at the day of Jesus Christ. Philippians 1:6

Prayer

Lord, I invite you to work in me today. It feels messy and uncomfortable, but please use it for something good. Grow my faith. Let me come to a place where I can comfort and encourage others. Whatever good you have in mind for the future, please bring it to completion. Don't leave me here, but may you please walk closely with me in the process. Amen.

According to this verse, God is...

Something I'm thankful for today:

Truth to Ponder

God is always at work in my life.

Prayers & Reflections

Lord, I feel...

Lord, I am hopeful that...

More Verses: Ephesians 2:10, Philippians 2:13

Truly, truly, I say to you, you will weep and lament, but the world will rejoice. You will be sorrowful, but your sorrow will turn to joy.
John 16:20

Prayer

Thank you, Lord, that you have overcome death. Thank you that I have the hope of eternity in your presence. Thank you that when I rejoice and praise you, I invite your goodness to be the focus of my thoughts. Lord, please take this sorrow that I'm experiencing and use it to draw me closer to you. May I come to know you in a deeper way as I run to you for comfort. Transform my grief into something meaningful.
In Jesus' name I ask. Amen.

According to this verse, God is...

Something I'm thankful for today:

Truth to Ponder

God can restore our joy.

Prayers & Reflections

Lord, I feel...

Things that have made me smile this week:

More Verses: Psalm 51:12, Isaiah 61:3, Psalm 69:29

When the cares of my heart are many, your consolations cheer my soul. Psalm 94:19

Prayer

Lord, My heart hurts. Cheer my soul. Remind me of your love for me. Remind me of your goodness. Reveal yourself to me. Surround me with your beauty and grace. I need you, Lord.
In Jesus' name I ask. Amen.

According to this verse, God is...

Something I'm thankful for today:

Truth to Ponder

When knowing God is my deepest desire, he heals my heart.

Prayers & Reflections

Lord, I feel...

Lord, I experience your comfort when...

More Verses: Psalm 16:11, Psalm 23, Philippians 4:6

Where shall I go from your Spirit? Or where shall I flee from your presence?
Psalm 139:7

Prayer

Lord, Thank you that I'm never alone. Thank you that even when I don't feel your presence, you're still with me. Surprise me today with a reminder of your love for me. Let me see or hear or smell something that reassures me that you're near. Amen.

According to this verse, God is...

Something I'm thankful for today:

Truth to Ponder

Ask God to reveal himself today.

Prayers & Reflections

Lord, I feel...

I felt seen this week when...

More Verses: Psalm 145:18, Deuteronomy 31:6, Isaiah 41:10

See what kind of love the Father has given to us, that we should be called children of God; and so we are.

1 John 3:1

Prayer

Dear Loving Father, Your word says that you love me. That I'm family. That I have an inheritance in you. That I'm blessed by you. That you sent your son to die for my sins so I could spend eternity with you. Help me to truly understand the depths of your love for me. When I'm consumed by my sadness and pain, I struggle to see your truth. Help me to see and know. Amen.

According to this verse, God is...

Something I'm thankful for today:

Truth to Ponder

God loves us lavishly, even when we don't feel it.

Prayers & Reflections

Lord, I feel...

I felt loved this week when...

More Verses: Psalm 109:26, 1 John 4:9-10, Ephesians 3:17-19

Trust in the Lord with all your heart and do not lean on your own understanding. In all your ways acknowledge him, and he will make straight your paths.
Proverbs 3:5-6

Prayer

Lord, I struggle to trust you at times. I can't see you. I can't feel you. I believe, but please help my unbelief. Use this difficult season to grow my faith and for me to know you better. Comfort me with the truth that you'll direct me and that you have a good plan for me. Fill me with hope. In Jesus' name I ask. Amen.

According to this verse, God is...

Something I'm thankful for today:

Truth to Ponder

We are never outside of God's reach. Invite him to show the way forward.

Prayers & Reflections

Lord, I feel...

Lord, I trust you to...

More Verses: Psalm 9:10, Psalm 46:10, Psalm 28:7

You will seek me and find me, when you seek me with all your heart.
Jeremiah 29:13

Prayer

Lord, I need you. My energy in lacking. My thoughts are jumbled at times. My heart hurts. I struggle to make sense of things right now. This very prayer is my effort to seek you. Accept my offering, however meager, and come to me. Rescue me. Give me rest. Comfort me. Strengthen me. Make yourself known. Amen.

According to this verse, God is...

Something I'm thankful for today:

Truth to Ponder

God can always be found in Scripture.

Prayers & Reflections

Lord, I feel...

Lord, I saw evidence of you this week, when...

More Verses: Proverbs 8:17, 1 Chronicles 16:11, Psalm 40:16

And he said, "My presence will go with you,
and I will give you rest."
Exodus 33:14

Prayer

Lord, I long for rest. Rest from my thoughts and emotions. Rest from the demands of my life right now. I long for restful sleep at night. Lord, please refresh me right now - physically, spiritually, emotionally. Restore my soul. Help me to be still in your presence and give me a rest better than anything I've know.
In Jesus' name I ask. Amen.

According to this verse, God is...

Something I'm thankful for today:

Truth to Ponder

God is always with me and offers rest.

Prayers & Reflections

Lord, I feel...

Ways I can rest this week:

More Verses: Isaiah 26:3, John 14:27, Psalm 23

Rejoice in hope, be patient in tribulation, be constant in prayer.

Romans 12:12

Prayer

Lord, My prayer today is a reflection of my faith in you. I am seeking you in my need. I praise you as the sovereign one. I thank you for your mercy, grace and comfort. Lord, help me to remember your goodness and be filled with your hope. May prayer be my first response when I'm struggling. Amen.

According to this verse, God is...

Something I'm thankful for today:

Truth to Ponder

Prayer points us to hope and demonstrates our faith in God..

Prayers & Reflections

Lord, I feel...

My prayer for today:

More Verses: Isaiah 40:31, Romans 15:13, Psalm 31:24

Hear, O Lord, and be merciful to me! O Lord, be my helper! You have turned my mourning into dancing; you have loosed my sackcloth and clothed me with gladness.

Psalm 30:10-11

Prayer

Lord, Make something beautiful from my loss and grief. I struggle to even ask you because I can't fathom what that might be. But I ask with the smallest hint of faith. Lord, show me beauty and restore my joy. May I fully remember my child with warmth and affection but may I have hope that they are safe with you. Let me rejoice in your love and may you fill the ache in my heart. In Jesus' name I ask. Amen.

According to this verse, God is...

Something I'm thankful for today:

Truth to Ponder

God can turn my messy emotions into something beautiful.

Prayers & Reflections

Lord, I feel...

Lord, I see your goodness in the following ways:

More Verses: Isaiah 61:3, Ecclesiastes 3:1-8

Thoughts about this passage:

Beyond Day 40

O God, you are my God; earnestly I seek you; my soul thirsts for you; my flesh faints for you, as in a dry and weary land where there is no water. So I have looked upon you in the sanctuary, beholding your power and glory.

Because your steadfast love is better than life, my lips will praise you. So I will bless you as long as I live; in your name I will lift up my hands.

My soul will be satisfied as with fat and rich food, and my mouth will praise you with joyful lips, when I remember you upon my bed, and meditate on you in the watches of the night; for you have been my help, and in the shadow of your wings I will sing for joy.

My soul clings to you; your right hand upholds me.

Psalm 63: 1-8

Reflections:

Ways I progressed in the past 40 days:

Next Steps:

Closing Thoughts

What we suffer now is nothing compared to the glory he will reveal to us later. (Romans 8:18) And while it may take time for us to see and believe this statement, it is indeed true. My prayer for you is to experience his goodness and glory in your life. May you have such a hunger and thirst for him that everything in this world fades in comparison. May you experience his redemption and restoration and may you continue to seek him until that time. Blessings to you in the journey ahead. Keep pressing into God's love. And may you know the comfort and peace of his presence.

Made in the USA
Middletown, DE
14 April 2023